I0098314

Lord, Teach Me

to be a

Blessing!

Lord, Teach Me

to be a

Blessing!

Dr. Cassundra White-Elliott

This book is a work of non-fiction. However, in some of the testimonies, individuals' names have either been changed or omitted to protect personal privacy.

All scripture are taken from the King James Version of the Holy Bible, unless otherwise noted.

Published by CLF Publishing, Inc.

Copyright © 2012 by Cassundra White-Elliott. All rights reserved. No portion of this book may be reproduced, stored in a retrieval system, or transmitted by any form or any means electronically, photocopied, recorded, or any other except for brief quotations in printed reviews, without the prior permission of the publisher.

ISBN # 978-0-9857372-0-7

Printed in the United States of America.

DEDICATIONS

This book is dedicated to the memory of my godson Deli
Manning, who departed this life on May 16, 2012,

and

my long-time friend of over 16 years, Keisha R. Williams,
who departed this life on May 19, 2012.

Their memories will forever live on in my life.

ACKNOWLEDGEMENTS

Special thanks are given to all of you who took the time to share your testimonies with me. Your experiences will change lives across the nation, from this decade to the next.

Table of Contents

Introduction

Today's society teaches individuals to look out for themselves and place themselves first above others. This train of thought has led people to adopt the "Me-Me" syndrome, where they profess "Me, Myself, and I" as most important. Everywhere we look, we see people competing against one another for fame and fortune, trying to outdo one another, rather than helping one another to get ahead.

The bible, however, does not share this same sentiment. Acts 20:35 declares, *"I have shewed you all things, how that so laboring ye ought to support the weak, and to remember the words of the Lord Jesus, how he said, 'It is more blessed to give than to receive'."* This book will demonstrate how important it is to put others first, and in doing so, you will receive your just reward from the Lord.

The bible says in Luke 6:38, *"Give, and it shall be given unto you; good measure, pressed down, and shaken together, and running over, shall men give into your bosom. For with the same measure that ye mete withal it shall be measured to you again."*

Let us examine each component of this verse in order to understand the message contained within. First and most important is the very first word in the verse: *"Give."* The comma after "give" followed by the conjunction "and" illustrates the preceding word is a complete thought. *"Give"* is a complete thought and needs no explanation. It is a clear instruction.

The subject of the instruction is not written; rather, it is implied: you. The speaker, Jesus, is speaking directly to the reader. He is telling the reader to give. His statement causes the following questions arise: To whom are we to give? And, what are we to give? I will answer these questions as simply as the statement was given. We are to give to others. The list of others is non-exhaustive, so I will not attempt to list all persons you could possibly give to because no one is excluded. And, if you examine the words and the structure of the verse directly preceding, you will understand what Jesus is asking us to render.

Luke 6:37 states, *"Judge not, and ye shall not be judged: condemn not, and ye shall not be condemned: forgive, and ye shall be forgiven:"* Jesus is informing us of the danger of judging others. When we judge, we place ourselves in a position to be judged as well. Notice the first full statement of the verse ends with a colon. In this case, the colon indicates a further explanation follows. To ensure the disciples' understanding, Jesus uses different conditions to give the same type of illustration. He tells us if we condemn, we set ourselves up to be condemned.

Therefore, it is to best to refrain from condemning others, unless we desire the same judgment. After the second statement, another colon appears. This colon has the same function as the first. The explanation that follows informs us to have a heart of forgiveness, and, as a result, we will be forgiven. For the third time, a colon appears at the end of the statement and leads us into Luke 6:38.

Consequently, we can safely extrapolate that the statement that follows is an explanation of the previous. Jesus is telling us to give forgiveness. However, I firmly believe that the meaning is not limited to forgiveness. Also, "give" does not only apply to monetary gifts, as often inferred over the pulpit. Now that we know giving is not limited to forgiveness or money, what else can we give?

We can give unto others our talents and our time, in addition to our money and our emotions of love, kindness, peace, and happiness, etc.

The second portion of the verse says, *"and it shall be given unto you."* When the instruction to *give* has been properly responded to, God is obligated to fulfill the second part of the verse. Numbers 23:19 says, *"God is not a man, that he should lie; neither the son of man, that he should repent: hath he said, and shall he not do it? or hath he spoken, and shall he not make it good?"* Your action prompts God's reaction. God's reaction is the blessing flow. He would not have you give and not make sure you are a receiver as well.

However, it is important that we do not place further expectations on God that He did not promise to deliver. For example, God did not say that the person you give to would be the same one who blesses you in return. Many people judge what another should do for them based on what they have done for the person. It is important to remember that God is the giver.

James 1:17 states, *"Every good gift and every perfect gift is from above, and cometh down from the Father of lights, with whom is no variableness, neither shadow of turning."* All good gifts flow through God. When He prompts us to give, He is simply using us as a vessel to bless someone else. The same is true when someone gives to us. Therefore, when we give, we should thank God for using us to be a blessing. When we receive, we should not only thank the person, but we should also thank God for the person's obedience for being willing to be used of Him. Foremost though, we should thank God for His gift.

The third part of the verse explains the second part. We understand the second part informs us of God's obligation as a result of His own Word. *"Good measure, pressed down, and shaken together, and running over"* tells us how God is going to give unto us.

Measurements are used to apportion a specific amount. Here, we are not told the specific amount, nor are we told what the measuring tool will be. We are only told it will be good. And, He says the gift will be pressed down. Think about the laundry basket you use daily to place your dirty clothes in. When the basket becomes full and it is not yet laundry day, you begin to push the clothes down into the basket. The act of pressing down is for one purpose and one purpose only: to place more clothes into the basket until it is time to take them out. As God is giving back to you, He presses the gift down, so He will have room to add more.

While God is giving you a good portion and pressing it down to add more, He also shakes the gift. Shaking permits the uneven pieces the opportunity to fit together better, resulting in less unused spaces in the receptacle. At this point, the receptacle used to house God's blessing is now full. There is no more room for any more to fit. However, God does not cease His giving. He continues to pour out until the gift is running over, thus providing us with more than enough for ourselves as well as enough to give others. The gifts that God blesses us with are not only for us. They are meant to be shared.

Continuing to explore the verse, the next portion states, *"shall men give into your bosom."* This portion of the verse explains the medium through which we will be blessed. God will use men to operate through. Blessings do not fall from the sky. They are transported through mediums: men. When we are willing and are submitted unto God, we avail ourselves as willing vessels to be used of God. God uses us to bless those He wants to receive special blessings.

For example, when we get a raise at work, God operates through our boss. When we go to a store and expect to pay a certain price for an item but the cashier enters a coupon on our behalf, God is using the cashier to bless us. When we have loving parents who nurture, teach, and love us,

God is blessing us through our parents. When we take care of the widows, orphans, and elderly, God is blessing them through us.

The last portion of the verse states, *"For with the same measure that ye mete withal it shall be measured to you again."* To mete is to distribute by or as if by measure, to allot. Earlier, I stated, "God reacts to your actions. God's reaction is the blessing flow." Blessings flow in different amounts.

Think of it this way, if you turn on a faucet, water will pour forth. However, if you only turn the handle slightly, a small amount of water will dispense. But, it you turn the handle to full capacity, much more water will dispense. Your giving is the turning of the handle. If you limit how much you turn, you are in essence limiting how much God measures back to you. On the other hand, if you give freely without reservation, God will bless you in the same manner. Consequently, although God is the giver of the blessings, you are the one who determines how your blessings flow back to you. This principal is also echoed in II Corinthians 9:6, *"But this I say, He which soweth sparingly shall reap also sparingly; and he which soweth bountifully shall reap also bountifully."*

The Lord wants us to live an abundant life. He makes this clear in John 10:10 when He contrasts Satan's intent for us and His intent. Satan walks about the earth roaring as a lion with the purpose of stealing from us, killing our hopes and dreams, and destroying our future. Jesus, on the other hand, came so we may have a more abundant life: a life that is full in every aspect.

When we accept God's plan for our lives, we can have a life of abundance. To do this, we must completely eradicate any hint of the world's mentality from our minds. God's word says, *"As a man thinketh, so is he"* (Proverbs 23:7), and *"Do not be conformed to this world, but be ye transformed by the renewing of your mind"* (Romans 12:2).

Following this introduction is a collection of testimonies. Revelations 12:10-11 discusses Satan's defeat and how he was overcome by the blood of the lamb (Jesus' shed blood on the cross) and the words of believers' testimonies. By reading the testimonies and the comments that follow each one, Satan can be defeated in the battlefield of the mind, thereby extinguishing the "Me-me" mentality and replacing it with an "other-centered" mentality.

Testimonies
of
God's Goodness

(Demonstrating the Cycle of Giving)

"Compassionate Giving"

*"But whoso hath this world's good, and seeth his brother have
need, and shutteth up his bowels of compassion from him, how
dwelleth the love of God in him?"*
I John 3:17

Janice is a known giver. She gives out of the abundance
of her heart whenever she is able. As a result of her
generosity towards others, the Lord saw fit to return a
blessing unto her (as promised in His word). The annual tax
season had arrived, and Janice was anxious to complete her
taxes; however, when she began to use the online tax
programs, the results were not favorable. Not being
satisfied, she put off filing her taxes for several weeks.
After some time had passed, she decided to go ahead and
face the music. After arriving to her tax appointment and
spending time with the agent who entered her numbers into
the computer, she was pleasantly surprised and overjoyed
by the results. The amount of the return was much, much
more than she ever anticipated.

Once Janice received her money, she did not forget the
Lord or His people. She immediately began to seek out
those she could bless. She blessed members of her
immediate family and her church. But, she did not stop
there. In planning for an upcoming women's retreat, there

were several women who desired to go but who were not able to due to their financial circumstances. Janice immediately compiled a mental list of whom she could afford to pay for, so she could be a blessing to other women. In the end, others began to make monetary contributions to be a blessing as well, and many women were blessed to attend the retreat.

****

Compassionate givers are those who give from the compassion of their heart. No one, but the Holy Spirit, compels the people to give. They see a need and fill it by graciously looking outside of themselves to see the needs of others. Vainglory has no place in these types of situations. Givers do not anticipate receiving accolades from the recipients. Instead, they are content with doing what needs to be done.

"One Hand Washes the Other"

"For God is not unrighteous to forget your work and labour of love, which ye have shewed toward his name, in that ye have ministered to the saints, and do minister."
Heb. 6:10

A faithful evangelist recently began to pastor a church. As she began to lay the foundation of the church, building it from the ground up, God blessed her with an armor bearer who has a heart to serve. After a year of serving tirelessly, the pastor decided to take a well-needed vacation, along with a group of her friends.

Suddenly, one of her friends was unable to take the vacation trip, leaving her place available for another passenger. The Holy Spirit quickened the pastor's spirit, and the pastor decided to pay for the open spot and take her armor bearer on the trip. Just as she needed a small break from her labor of love, she knew that the same was true for her assistant. Here, the armor bearer gave her time to the pastor, and God allowed her to receive her just reward- a well-deserved trip.

####### *******

The Lord tells us in Matthew 11:28, *"Come to Me, all you who labor and are heavy laden, and I will give you rest."* God has promised us that we can rest in Him. After

21

we have labored in the vineyard, we must be wise to allow our physical bodies to rest so that we are not weary in well doing.

When we see a co-laborer in Christ working tirelessly and is not able to take his/her rest in the Lord, we should step in and do what we can to give the person a break. We may not be able to send the person on a trip, but we may be able to take him/her out for dinner, to a movie, or even for ice cream. Our acts of kindness can go a long way and give the person the break he/she needs. The break we provide could save the person from getting to his/her breaking point. Never underestimate the power of a kind act.

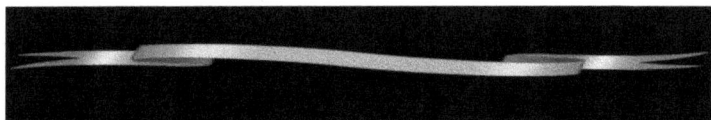

"A Heart of Compassion"

"Put on then, as God's chosen ones, holy and beloved, compassionate hearts, kindness, humility, meekness, and patience."
Col. 3:12 (ESV)

Acts of compassion are usually witnessed as interactions that transpire between one adult and another or from an adult to a child. Conversely, many compassionate acts of children go unnoticed by man. God, on the other hand, sees all and knows all. Jeremiah 23:24 declares, *"Can any hide himself in secret places that I shall not see him? saith the LORD."*

The following testimony will provide an example of acts committed by an adolescent who grew into a mighty woman of God because God touched her life at a young age. Growing up, Karen and her siblings were subjected to a single mother who was addicted to drugs. To Karen's surprise Lisa, another young girl, who lived on the same street, also had a mother who was addicted to drugs. The difference between Karen's and Lisa's mothers was Karen's mother was home in the evenings with her children; whereas, Lisa's mother would arrive home late each evening.

The absence of Lisa's mother caused Lisa to be locked outside of the house. Day after day, Lisa sat outside without shelter or food until her mother returned home. Karen befriended Lisa and offered her an opportunity for shelter inside Karen's home, so she would not be subjected to cold and/or inclement weather and unsafe conditions. Karen imagined what her friend was going through and offered a helping hand. However, Karen's mother was not

23

compassionate. She only permitted Lisa into her home on a single occasion. She did want to be involved or take the role of a concerned neighbor. Although Karen was not permitted to allow Lisa into the house after that particular day, Karen made sure Lisa did not go hungry due to her mother's absence. Each day that Lisa sat outside, Karen took her food to eat. This act of compassion lasted for years.

As time drew on, Karen and her siblings progressed from elementary school into junior high school and later to high school. Throughout these years, their mother continued to be an avid drug user. In her drug-addicted state, she had several boyfriends who would visit her in the family home. Not all of the mother's boyfriends or their friends were upstanding characters. One of the boyfriend's friends showed pornography to Karen and her sister in an attempt to get them interested in sex. One girl told their mother about the incident, and the mother promptly dismissed the friend from the home. There were a few more incidents along these lines, but Karen and her siblings were covered by God's divine protection and were never sexually or physically abused by any of their mother's boyfriends or friends.

As an adult, Karen now recognizes the role God played in her life from the time of a child. She continues to assist others when she is able. She looks to be a blessing rather than looking to receive a blessing. This is a characteristic of Christ; one that He desires all followers to adopt.

****

Whether you are a child or an adult who is reading this book, you are not too young or too old to see to the needs of another person. Lend a helping hand rather than turning a blind eye or a deaf ear. Someone's very life may depend on what you do next.

If you are a child and you see a person in need, the best thing to do is to go to an adult and let him/her know the situation. The adult can guide you in what is best to do in the situation. Talking to an adult can prevent any possible problems from occurring.

"From Our Lips to God's Ears"

"Trust in the LORD with all thine heart; and lean not unto thine own understanding. In all thy ways acknowledge him, and he shall direct thy paths."
Prov. 3:5-6

Mr. and Mrs. Green served as associate pastors at their home church for four years. In serving the Lord under the leadership of the senior pastor, Mr. Green worked alongside the senior pastor, while Mrs. Green worked diligently as the Children's Ministry Director as she re-established the children's church that had fallen by the wayside. Years later, the Greens placed their membership at another church and have continued to serve the Lord faithfully in the ministry as they stand alongside the pastor and his wife, the associate pastor. During these times of being faithful to their calling, the Greens have seen the favor of the Lord in their lives. For example, when the Greens wanted to build their dream house, they were blessed to do so. They purchased a lot in Azusa and watched as the home of their dreams was erected.

During the five years that they lived in their home, they had the misfortune of going into foreclosure three times due to a promise from the lender that their loan would be refinanced. Unfortunately, the Greens did not know that the lender was in Chapter 13 'Bankruptcy,' and they continued to be given false promises. Upon the last occurrence of foreclosure, the Greens attempted to save their home once again via a phone call. Mrs. Green was led by the Holy Spirit to call a former lender who told them just what they needed to hear. They knew everything was in the hands of God.

Mr. Green decided one day to go to the credit union looking to purchase a car. As he walked into the credit union, the credit union's CEO walked out of his office, with his hand extended toward Mr. Green, and said, "Hello, Mr. Brown." Mr. Green did not know what to make of this because he was dropping in without an appointment and obviously he was being addressed by the wrong name. He gave the CEO his actual name, informed him that he did not have an appointment, and told him why he had come in that particular day. The CEO told him to come into his office so he could have an in-depth look into his situation. After playing around with the numbers on the computer, the CEO regrettably informed Mr. Green that he was unable to save his home from foreclosure. On the other hand, the CEO had a bit of good news as well. He told Mr. Green that he had several houses on the market, and Mr. Green could have any one of his choice.

After viewing pictures of the homes online in the CEO's office, Mr. Green promptly called his wife and asked her if she was attached to their home. She replied, "I'm not attached to anything." Soon afterwards, Mr. and Mrs. Green went to view some of the homes that the CEO had shown Mr. Green, and they chose a house that had the same color scheme of their present home. The only thing that was different was their current home did not have the same flooring as the 'new' home. What was great about that was the flooring in the 'new' home was the exact flooring and kitchen counter tops that Mrs. Green had desired but was unable to afford.

Soon afterwards, the Greens moved into their new home without any money down and no credit check. The CEO had taken the house off the market until they were ready to move in, which was about four months later. Also, their new mortgage payment was three times less than the previous one. It was as though they had their dream home all over again but with less hassle. The Greens did also purchase a car through the credit union, which was their original plan the day Mr. Green walked in the credit union. The Greens' testimony demonstrates that God will truly give us the desires of our hearts (Prov. 3:5-6).

****

Although the Greens were in foreclosure, they were not looking for a handout from anyone. They were going about their way and serving the Lord as they had been commissioned to do. But God knew their situation, and He had a ram in the bush. He knew the desires of their hearts, and He directed their paths in such a way that would lead them to the person He would ultimately use to bless them.

God has a blessing for all givers. When He orders our steps, we need to be obedient to His direction, so we can walk right into our destiny!

"A Co-Worker's Advice"

"Hear counsel, and receive instruction, that thou mayest be wise in thy latter end."
Prov. 19:20

While working at the Sherriff's department, Samantha's coworker advised her to obtain disability insurance.

Agreeing that disability insurance was good to have, Samantha filled out the necessary paperwork. Years later, Samantha was hurt on the job and subsequently taken off work. Afterwards, even more years passed and Samantha found herself at home and unemployed. One day as she was reviewing her bank statements (something she never did), she saw a charge of $151.

Immediately, Samantha called her bank and learned that the company withdrawing the money on a monthly basis was called Metlife. They had been withdrawing the money for years. The name of the company was unfamiliar to Samantha because when she first applied for disability insurance, the company had a different name. It is possible that Metlife bought her policy from the original holder. Nevertheless, Samantha called Metlife and explained her situation. The company's first response was, "We have no record of you." She responded, "That's strange because you have been taking $151 from my checking account monthly for years."

After a few more minutes of discussion, the agent located her information and told her that she was indeed insured. She immediately filed a claim, as she had been hurt on the job and had been off for three or four years. As a result of her claim being filed, she was promptly sent a check for $68,000. Upon receiving the check, she gave her tithes of ten percent to her church, and she also gave an offering. Samantha believes this gift from God was a result of being a faithful tithe payer and for always having a giving heart.

****

God pays great dividends when we are obedient to His Word. When we enter into a covenant with God, and we honor our word, God will honor is word.

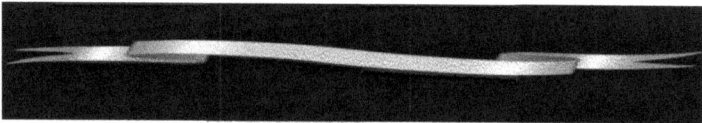

"Resting in the Lord"

"Rest in the LORD, and wait patiently for him."
Psalm 37:7

After working for over forty years, in various fields, with over twenty years in Information Technology Systems, the wear and tear of commuting and twelve-hour days for the last three years had begun to take its toll on Jim. When the renewal time for the yearly contract approached, Jim was faced with a hard decision. Would he dare turn down the contract for the next year, denying an opportunity to do what he loved, but get much-needed physical and mental rest? Or, would he accept the new contract and continue to work in his beloved field, but continue to allow his health to suffer by commuting 85 miles one way? Jim was faced with a hard choice.

Even after speaking extensively to his wife about the choices that lay before him, Jim was yet in limbo. At one point, he decided he would retire, while at another point he was not so sure. Leaving the situation in God's hands, Jim awaited the new contract. He decided if the company offered him a reasonable salary increase, he would stay for another year. However, if there was not a salary increase, he would seriously consider leaving. So, Jim's decision hung in the balance as he continued to go to work day after day.

Finally, the day of reckoning came, and Jim learned his fate. His job did not give him a raise; they did not even keep his pay rate the same. Instead, they decided to close his position leaving him with two choices: find another job or retire. He chose the latter of the two. Today, Jim is relishing and basking in his retirement. He is feeling and looking better. God truly blessed him by closing a door and allowing him to rest in the Lord! Now, Jim can be a blessing to others because he has more time and energy to give.

****

Many times when we are faced with a decision, we may find ourselves in limbo not knowing which way to go. The available options may seem to be great for different reasons. However, when we use godly wisdom, refrain from hasty decision making, and allow God to order our steps, we always come out on the winning end.

"God's Will for My Life"

"And above all things have fervent charity among yourselves: for charity shall cover the multitude of sins."
I Peter 4:8

A couple of years ago, Kelly was in her place of business when Gerry, a stranger, walked in. After the two exchanged pleasantries, they immediately felt a connection. Eventually, the two began dating. Approximately three weeks later, Kelly invited Gerry to be her guest at church. Gerry consented and began to attend church services with Kelly on a regular basis. Six months into the relationship, the couple began marriage counseling.

After three months of marriage counseling, Kelly told Gerry she thought it would be best if they both spent some time alone with God and not with each other. Her intent was for both of them to go into their secret and quiet places to commune with the Lord. Gerry did not like Kelly's idea one bit. He told her that he was not in agreement with her idea and that he wanted to move forward with the relationship at that point rather than take the suggested break. Because Kelly had a made-up mind to seek and hear from God, she did not push the issue when Gerry decided to end the relationship and walk away.

Not a month later, another young lady, Felicia, came to the church. After some time passed, Gerry and Felicia began dating. Felicia learned of Gerry and Kelly's relationship, and she began to taunt Kelly by sitting next to her and making snide remarks about how Kelly let her Boaz get away. Two months later, Gerry and Felicia were married. However, it was not a marriage that would last.

After six months of dreadful matrimony, Gerry and Felicia separated. During the time of the marriage and afterwards, Kelly had many opportunities to minister to Felicia, and she did just that. Through her own hurt and pain of the broken relationship with Gerry, Kelly stood with the strength God poured into her.

In return for receiving God's healing virtue, Kelly poured healing and strength into Felicia, who then too was suffering from a broken relationship: a failed marriage. Kelly could have turned a blind eye or a deaf ear to Felicia, but instead, she put her hurt, disappointment and pride aside to see to the need of her sister in Christ. Through Kelly's love and obedience to God, she was able to minister to Felicia and show her sisterly love as well as show brotherly love to Gerry. As time went on, the two women developed a friendship. Now, they can lean on one another in their times of need.

****

A relationship is formed when two people come together in some type of agreement or connection. The two people may be husband and wife, brother and sister, parent and child, coworkers or friends. However, regardless of the type of relationship the two have with one another, relationship troubles can arise and cause emotional stress upon one or both of the parties.

Today, most people do not want to get involved with other people's problems, especially when it has to do with their home life. However, without intervening and prying into the personal details of the problem, we can be of comfort to the ailing person(s) by just lending a shoulder to cry on or an ear to hear.

Sometimes the person may not want to talk about anything. He or she may just want to be in your presence. Rather than avoiding people who are hurting, we should seek them out and let them know that we care. Sometimes, they just feel alone and need another person to be there to let them know they are special and important.

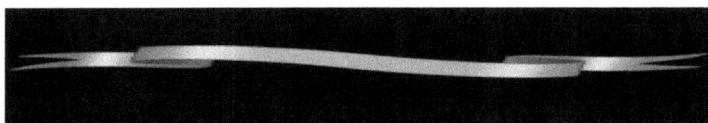

"Loosed from the Devil's Grip"

"And having spoiled principalities and powers, he made a shew of them openly, triumphing over them in it."
Col. 2:15

(The following testimony, shared by Jose Garcia, is in his own words.)

The accounts that I am about to reveal are all part of my testimony, which God has given me to share with anyone who will hear it. This testimony is not a boast or in any way shape or form shared for the purpose of self-glorification; rather, it is shared all for the honor and glory of the Lord Jesus Christ, my savior. These events have not been altered or modified; they are very real, as are the forces that are involved. It has been about a year since my transformation, and yet I'm still in awe of how the merciful Lord came to change my life.

My heart, before the cleansing of the Lord, was filled with deceit, lust, and perversion, just to name a few of the demons that had a tight grip on me. I was highly addicted to pornography and masturbation. I was masturbating day in and day out, giving into the pleasures of my flesh. This, as well as the pornography, became routine for me and I instilled, to relieve myself of the guilt, in my mind that it was "normal."

My eyes now having been unveiled, I now know God was reaching out to me through many outlets, such as television shows based on *Hell* that I would often times come across as I flipped through the channels. Hell has always been a frightening subject to me because I grew up hearing about hell, and thus, I believe that such a place of indescribable torment exists. These types of television shows only made my guilt consume me to the soul. I knew the way I was living my life was only leading me to one place, that place of damnation. These television shows were the spark that God utilized to ignite His life-changing plot in me.

Soon after that particular television show, I found myself wanting to seek the things of the Lord more and more. At first, I had a hard time picking up the Holy Bible and reading it. This was not because I did not want to but because of my own lack of understanding it. So I looked for other outlets to begin my walk toward my salvation, and I found it in the author Mary K. Baxter. I began to read one of her books entitled *A Divine Revelation of the Spirit Realm*. As I read this book, I began to see how the devil had been using all of my addictions as chains to hold me down, and had it not been for my savior Jesus Christ, he would have very well dragged me to hell! But the devil knew he would soon release his entire grip on my soul; thus, as I was reading one day, he began to feed my mind perverse thoughts which began to lead to temptation.

As I was reading, I began to think to myself, "Damn, I want to masturbate! Ok, I'll go into the restroom after I finish this chapter." To this day, it blows my mind how I could be reading a book inspired by the Lord and at the same time be thinking such perverse things! That is a witness of the devil's power and his strong influence on us. His power, however, does not even come close to the power of my Lord and savior Jesus Christ! So at that moment as I was thinking such perversion, I put the book down and began to pray. I said, "Lord please! I don't want to do these things anymore!" At that very instant, all temptation fled from me! The urge and thought of masturbation was far from me! I picked the book back up and continued reading.

At that moment in time, it was not revealed to me how God had transformed me that very instant. It wasn't until later that same day that I began to notice things within me were different. Before my transformation, I was a very foul-mouthed person. I would use any little opportunity I could to curse and use offensive language. But that day, my ears could not stand the sound of such foul language. I would come across people who would use foul language in my presence, and I would literally cringe! I could not bear to hear such things! When night came, it did not once cross my mind to watch pornography or masturbate, which was amazing to me because that had become routine to me! The devil, however, was far from giving up.

That night as I sat on my couch watching television, a great fear came over me. I didn't know why I was afraid, but it was a fear that I had never felt before, and I felt a sense of hopelessness. Immediately, my attention focused on some DVD movies I had in my room. Particularly the ones of a television series entitled *Tales from the Crypt.* Before my transformation, I was highly addicted to this television series and loved it so much that it would anger me when my dad, who is a follower of Christ as well, would throw those DVD's in the trash. I always thought to myself, "What's the big deal with a little gore, murder and vengeance? It's not like I'm going to go out on a murderous spree!" But that particular night, I didn't think twice when something instilled in my heart to remove those DVD's from my room. I knew right there and then it was the Lord.

So without hesitation, I immediately sprang up off my couch and knelt down to get the DVD's from within my television stand. As I got back up to my feet, I felt a force push me back causing me to fall back on a massage bed that is in my room! I knew I hadn't lost my balance and almost instantly the thought demons were unhappy with me almost as if to say, "Sit down! You aren't throwing anything away!" came to my mind. I immediately picked myself back up, DVD's in hand, and walked out to my front yard where my garbage bin is located. It was about one in the morning, and the entire street that I live on was quiet with no one else around.

As I opened the garbage bin and began to break the DVD's, that same fear that I had felt moments earlier in my room came over me once again. It felt as if though someone was watching me even though there was no one around! I felt quite paranoid looking in all directions, but I simply prayed until the last of the DVD's was finally shattered. I walked back into my room and immediately felt at peace. The hopelessness and fear had been lifted from the room.

The following day, I told my mom everything that had happened, and she, in turn, told my dad. That night my dad invited a couple from his church to pray for me because that was the day I had decided it was time to rededicate myself to God.

That night, as we were in prayer, I dropped to my knees and was walked through a prayer. The pastor placed his hands on me as well as my dad. As soon as my dad placed his hand on me, I felt an electrifying warmth I had never experienced, and at that instant, we both began to weep as we prayed. I knew right then and there that the Lord had overshadowed us with His holy presence. There are no words that can describe the happiness that is felt when God dwells within someone!

That night was the beginning of a chain of blessings that the Lord granted me. From my dad and I reconciling our long tarnished father/son relationship to God replenishing me with His Holy Spirit and allowing me the power to speak to share this testimony with my older brother, which in turn led him back on the path to the Lord. I now understand the things of the Lord because He has been gracious enough to let them be known to me. I know with all my being that the Lord has begun His plan with my life! He has not only given me that which I did not have: love, patience, wisdom, and freedom, but He has allowed me to share it with all whom I come in contact with.

I am one of many living testimonies of what God has to offer and how through His gracious giving I now too can give. I could not give what I did not have, but since the Lord came into my heart, I have found myself giving more than I knew I ever had in me to give. I have spoken to many people sharing my testimony and giving words of encouragement that God has given unto me to share with them resulting in many of them turning and/or returning to Christ. I have not only been forgiven, but I have also been given the calling to give what the Lord has and continues to instill in me. Giving me that which I so longed for and fully need and demonstrating His beautiful attributes through every deed.

****

Sexual sins have a tendency to create strongholds in the lives of most people who get entangled in them. Without will power and the strength of the Lord, some people stay in bondage forever, not ever knowing how to break free. Sexual sins are frowned upon throughout the church and throughout society. As a result, most people who are bound by them will not admit their struggles.

Twelve-step programs throughout the nation have as their first step: admit a problem exists. When we desire to be released from a stronghold, we must call the demon by name and address it. The longer we sweep the problem under the rug, the longer we will be plagued by it.

Jose is a brave young man who stepped outside of himself and sought help from the Lord. Like him, there are others who suffer in silence. Pray for their immediate release from the enemy's grip, for they too can be delivered.

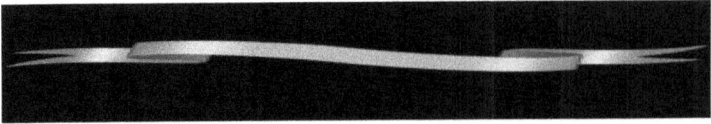

"Reaping God's Blessings"

"Be not deceived; God is not mocked: for whatsoever a man soweth, that shall he also reap. For he that soweth to his flesh shall of the flesh reap corruption; but he that soweth to the Spirit shall of the Spirit reap life everlasting."
Galatians 6:7-8

Growing up in Congo, Africa, Nathalie Banda and her nine siblings grew up in poverty-stricken conditions. There was little to eat and not a variety of clothes to wear. As a student, Nathalie only had one uniform to wear. She had to wash her uniform daily in order to have a fresh uniform the next day. When Nathalie became a young adult, she became a hairdresser. This was her means of an income. However, it did not solve her problems. She still suffered from poverty. But God has a plan for those who walk in faith.

One day while Nathalie was sitting in church, the pastor took up an offering and said, "If you give, God will see to your needs." At the time, Nathalie only had one dollar. This is all she had period. There was no money at home, in the bank, or under the mattress. Nathalie, walking in faith, obeyed the voice of her pastor and gave her last dollar. When she went home that evening, she went to bed hungry, as she had no food in the house.

Three days later, Nathalie's aunt, who lives in the United States sent her $450 and told her to go to Cameroon because she had set up an interview for Nathalie to come to the United States to live. Nathalie did as her aunt instructed and not long after, she came to the United States to live. She has been here now for a total of eight years. Now that she is here, she has not forgotten her parents or her siblings who still reside in her home country. She does all she can to send money and resources on a monthly basis, even though she now has two children of her own. By having a heart to give, Nathalie has continued to reap the Lord's blessings.

****

When Nathalie's pastor spoke the word of God and she walked in obedience to what he said, the Lord opened up a whole new world for Nathalie of which she could only have dreamed. Ephesians 3:20 says, *"Now unto him that is able to do exceeding abundantly above all that we ask or think, according to the power that worketh in us."*

We need to have that bold type of faith, where we are not moved by our circumstances to fear, but we instead take a step or leap of faith. We must know within our spirit that God is a god of His word. He is not a man that He should lie (Numbers 23:19).

Our faith is what is going to make the difference in our circumstances. Think about the woman, in the bible, who had the issue of blood for twelve years. She was healed when she touched the hem of Jesus' garment because of the belief she held that He *could* actually heal her. It was not the touching that healed her; it was her faith that healed her.

So, when we develop our faith and exercise it, we will see the blessings of the Lord come alive in our lives. Remember, faith without works is dead (James 2:17).

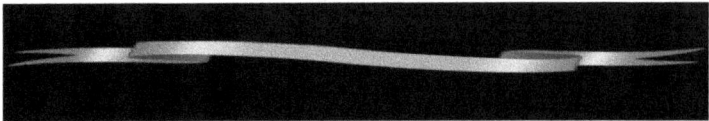

"A Rare Occasion"

"Therefore all things whatsoever ye would that men should do to you, do ye even so to them: for this is the law and the prophets."
Matt. 7:12

One summer when Vanessa's teaching load was light, she was unable to pay her car payment. One evening when she took her sons to football practice, while talking to one of her friends, she learned that her friend was experiencing the same trial. When Vanessa inquired of her friend how much her car note was, she learned her friend's note was half the amount of her own car note. It just so happened that Vanessa had the money needed to cover her friend's car note, so she graciously gave her friend the money. Her friend did not understand why Vanessa would give her money when she needed money herself. In an attempt to explain, Vanessa said, "I don't have enough money to pay my car note, but I have enough to pay yours. It does not make sense for both notes to go unpaid."

A year later, Vanessa needed to travel out of state for a book signing. The morning she was to leave would also be payday. She desired to leave money at her home for her children while she was away; however, due to the time of her flight she would be unable to go to the bank and get to the airport on time. As the day neared for her departure,

Vanessa was yet in limbo as to how to work out the best plan to make sure her children would have what they needed and be where she needed to be, at the same time. Unexpectedly, the same friend whom she gave the money for her car note called and said she had something for her, and she would stop by the next morning to bring it. Vanessa never expected the blessing that was in store for her.

When her friend arrived at her home, she extended her hand toward Vanessa. Vanessa reached out to receive what her friend held, and in her friend's hand was a roll of twenty dollar bills totaling $500. As Vanessa's eyes almost popped out of their sockets, her friend said these words, "This is all I could get out of the bank. I will get more on Monday morning." Vanessa replied, "Wow, thank you. Oh, I will be leaving early Monday morning." Her friend said, "I will be here before you leave with another $500." With the gift her friend bestowed upon her, Vanessa was able to leave town with peace of mind that her children would be taken care of and with traveling money, without using any money from the paycheck she would receive the day she departed.

****

We never know whom God is going to send to bless us. Blessings come in different packages and from the most unexpected people, even from single mothers of six children, like Vanessa's friend.

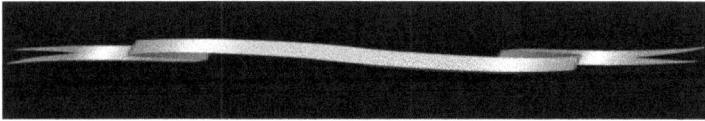

"In the Palm of the Lord's Hand"
"The earth is the LORD's, and the fulness thereof; the world, and they that dwell therein."
Psalm 24:1

In the world's time of economic recession, many teachers and professors across the nation have either been laid off or have experienced a decrease in their teaching load. Approximately three years ago, this had also been true for Dr. C who teaches for two community colleges and two universities. Due to the educational budget cuts in California, schools throughout the state had been dramatically impacted as courses and programs were cut. A decrease in workload generally means a decrease in wages.

During this time, Dr. C. became more involved in

teaching various sessions in her church. She first took on the responsibility of coordinating and teaching the women's group that meets every Wednesday night before bible study. Secondly, she began to teach the Adult Sunday School class every Sunday morning.

As a result of being diligent and generous with her time, the Lord saw fit to bless her abundantly in her career. Before the recession, she taught, on average, seven or eight courses at any given time. During the time of shortage, she was only teaching five classes on average, which is still a blessing because many others had lost their jobs completely.

Today, she is at times overwhelmed with classes as she continuously has an average of six to seven classes at a given time. Her blessings remind her of the scripture that says, "*The earth is the Lord's, and the fullness thereof*" (Psalm 24:1). God controls all of His creation, and this world system is not exempt. Satan may be the prince of the air and operate systems within the earth realm, but only God is omnipotent. He is the only one with complete power and complete authority.

****

Everyday burdens, worries and concerns can become

yokes of bondage around our necks if we succumb to them. We must, instead, hold fast to the following truth: God knows what we need before we ask (Matthew 6:8). When we keep this truth at the forefront of our minds, we loose the spirit of liberality in our lives. As a result, we are able to move freely doing those things God has called us to do. When we truly walk in our calling, God will ensure that each and every need we have is met.

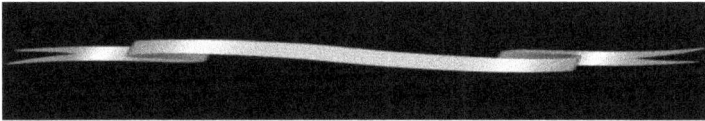

"A Life for a Life"

"Ye have heard that it hath been said, 'An eye for an eye, and a tooth for a tooth'."
Matthew 5:38

In 1994, Melanie accepted Jesus Christ as her Lord and Savior. Although she had accepted the gift of salvation, she had not fully committed her life unto Christ. For six years, she loved the Lord, but she struggled with having one foot in the world and the other foot out.

In 2000, she received a call from family saying her mother had been diagnosed with Lung Cancer and was comatose as a result of being overly medicated with pain medicine. Melanie immediately jumped in her car to drive the hour and a half long drive to get to the hospital where her mother had been admitted.

On the drive there, Melanie had a one and a half hour prayer where she cried out to God on her mother's behalf. She did not want to lose her mother. She was not ready to say goodbye. As she prayed a long fervent prayer, she began to beg and plead with God. The more she prayed, the more she begged God to spare her mother's life. Finally, she began to bargain with God, as so many people do when they find themselves in a situation over which they have no control. They know that God is omniscient, omnipresent, and omnipotent. They know while they are limited in what they can do, God is not. Melanie pleaded with God saying, "If you spare my mother's life, I will fully surrender to you. I will commit my complete life to you."

Arriving at the hospital, Melanie sat by her mother's bedside for three long days. The doctors had no hope of recovery for her mother and told the family she only had five days to live. On that third day, the family began to lose hope. As they walked into the hospital parking lot, they discussed going to a local liquor store and getting liquor to drink. Although Melanie, at the time, was an avid drinker, she had not lost hope in the God she had vowed to serve just three days before. Therefore, she was not the least bit interested in drinking. She was yet hopeful that God would hear her cry and heal her mother on her supposed deathbed.

While her family was yet discussing going to get a drink, an unknown man walked up to Melanie and called her by name. Melanie had never seen the man before, but because he called her by name, she gave him her attention. As the man began to speak to her, all the family members who were standing nearby departed, with exception of Melanie's younger sister. The man began to tell Melanie that the person who was inside the hospital would not die, that God would heal her, but God wanted something from Melanie. In her heart, Melanie knew that the man, who she now considers to be an angel of the Lord, came to confirm the words she spoke in her car on the way to the hospital. This was a wake-up call from God for Melanie to get her life on track.

As the man spoke, Melanie and her sister could feel the presence of the Lord move throughout the parking lot. While Melanie was familiar with the feeling of the presence of the Holy Spirit, her sister was not. The man walked over to the car where Melanie's sister was sitting and began to encourage her saying all was well and even though she did not understand what was going on and was fearful, she was to stick close by Melanie. The man continued to speak to both women telling them that the person who lay upon the deathbed would rise up in twenty-four hours, which at their calculation would be 6:15 pm the next evening.

Going back to her mother's side, Melanie continued praying. On day four, her mother's brother came into the hospital room and told Melanie and her sister to go to his house to shower, change clothes and get rest, for they had not showered or nearly slept for four days, after arriving to their mother's bedside. Following their uncle's instructions, the women went to their uncle's home. That night, they spent the night in their uncle's home.

The next day, in the evening, while the girls were yet at their uncle's home, the telephone rang. Melanie answered the phone and heard her uncle's voice on the other end. He said, "If you girls don't come down here and get your mother. She is awake and trying to get up and go to the bathroom." Melanie quickly relayed the information to her sister. Her sister said, "What time is it?" They quickly looked at the clock. The clock read 6:25pm. They figured from the time their mother awoke to the time the uncle called was about ten minutes. Therefore, their mother awoke within the twenty-four hour period as prophesied, and it was the fifth day, the day the doctors said she would expire.

Melanie gave herself to the Lord and received her mother back.

****

Melanie's testimony is similar to that of Hannah's, the mother of the prophet Samuel. In I Samuel, we read that Hannah, one of Elkanah's wives, was barren while another wife Peninnah had several children. Each year at the feast of Shiloh, Peninnah would taunt Hannah because their husband favored Hannah by giving her more meat than anyone. Peninnah would constantly berate Hannah about her barren condition and not giving Elkanah any children. Each year, the taunting grew worse.

Finally, in a desperate attempt to have her innermost

desire filled, Hannah cried out to God. Between her tears, she prayed and said to God, "If you give me a child, I will give him back to you," (I Samuel 1:26-2:11). At her request, she bore Samuel, her son. And when he was three years old, she took him to Eli the priest. She left Samuel with Eli, so he could serve the Lord.

Like Hannah, Melanie bargained with God. God gave her the desires of her heart, and she dedicated her own life to him.

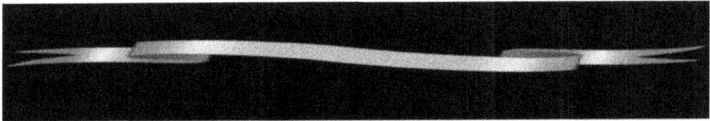

"Reaping God's Joy"

"Every man according as he purposeth in his heart, so let him give; not grudgingly, or of necessity: for God loveth a cheerful giver. And God is able to make all grace abound toward you; that ye, always having all sufficiency in all things, may abound to every good work."
II Corinthians 9:7-8

Mr. Dietrich, a deacon in the church, was home one day when he received a call from his brother, Melvin. Melvin had a financial need. Mr. Dietrich informed his brother that he had a little extra money, and he would bring it right over. When Mr. Dietrich arrived at Melvin's home, he gave his brother the money. Melvin was so thankful for his brother's kindness, and he wanted to do something for his brother in return. He said, "You know, you are the only one who responded to my need. I want you to take my food stamp card and go and get food for you and your wife." Mr. Dietrich was grateful for his brother's act of kindness, and he took the card.

As he drove away, he knew he and his wife did not need any food. They had plenty of food at home. So, he quickly began to think of someone he could bless. He thought of a close friend and his wife. He knew that times were tough, and they could benefit from a blessing of food. He called his friend and told him to have his wife make a grocery list, and he would send his own wife to get the list. His friend did just as he asked. After Mrs. Dietrich picked up the list, she and Mr. Dietrich went to the store to pick up the requested items.

After dropping the groceries off at his friends' home, he thought of another person who could possibly also benefit from receiving food. He then made a phone call to an old friend he had grown up with. When she answered the phone, he asked her how she was doing. After a brief hesitation, she said, "I am doing okay." Mr. Dietrich knew that the Holy Spirit had laid his friend on his mind, so he knew there was something she was not telling him.

Mr. Dietrich asked his friend again if everything was okay with her. She finally admitted that she did not have food in her refrigerator. Mr. Dietrich asked his wife once again to go grocery shopping. This time, she took their friend with her to get groceries. In the end, both households were blessed with food, Melvin was blessed with the finances he needed, and Mr. and Mrs. Dietrich were blessed with the joy of giving.

****

Often times, we may not be in need of the item with which we are blessed. In situations like this, we should not hoard the blessing, but we should give it to someone who really needs it. Remember, God uses men to bless others, and the blessing may come from one person to another in order to go to the intended recipient.

"God's Abundant Grace"

"For if by one man's offence death reigned by one; much more they which receive abundance of grace and of the gift of righteousness shall reign in life by one, Jesus Christ."
Romans 5:17

(The following testimony, shared by Sis. Merilyn Jolly, is in her own words.)

Since learning the principles of giving my time, talent and treasures, I have been tremendously blessed and am tremendously blessed.   According to some people's standards, being blessed is having a whole lot of money in the bank, a big beautiful house on the hills, near the beach or in a prestigious neighborhood with three cars parked in the garage. These things are okay, but having things is not what make you blessed.

To me, being blessed is having favor with God and with man and having all your needs being met for that day or for a particular time and purpose. Since I have been giving my tithes on a regular basis, I have seen God make ways and open doors like never before. When I gave my tithes sporadically, I was always in need and struggled to make ends meet. But when I made it up in my mind that I would give God what was due Him, I began to see an immediate change. Usually, I would run out of money before the next paycheck when I missed giving my tithes, but when I began to give on a regular basis, I had money when the next pay period came around. It may not have been a whole lot, but it was enough to do what I needed and wanted to do.

Some way and somehow, God would stretch what I had left over after giving my tithes and offerings. He would bless me through others. Sometimes people would just come up to me and put a few dollars in my hand-just because or they may have owed me money and was repaying me; other times, someone would buy me lunch or dinner thus saving me from spending what I had.

On one occasion, I had to pay my rent in addition to other bills that were due at that time, and I knew giving my tithes would cause me to fall short of what I needed. I was sitting in the choir stand when offering time came around, and I struggled as to whether or not to give my tithes. I made a decision that I was going to give my tithes and trust God to make a way for what I needed. I said, *"Father, I'm going to pay my tithes and you're just gonna' have to make a way for whatever else I need."* So, I gave my tithes. About two days later, I received back the amount of tithes that I gave on that Sunday plus some. Since then, I have been faithful in giving my tithes.

I even get blessed when I give of my time at the church. Only a few people know that being employed by the church does not bring you a big paycheck, but because I try to be faithful in giving of my time, God blesses me. People give me clothes and money, buy my lunch, and just give me stuff because they tell me I work so hard and diligently and never seem to complain. I try to be nice to people and treat them the way that I would want to be treated, but I also believe that God gives me favor with people and whatever you put out you get back.

I do programs and invitations outside of the regular church work that I do. Many times, I have more work than I can do at times, but God helps me to get it done. I try not to overcharge the clients because I am not trying to get rich off them. I always ask them their budget up front and try to stay within their budget. When it comes time for them to pay for the work, they always pay more than what I quoted them. I see this as a blessing from God.

On one occasion, I went to Carl's Jr. to purchase food. I gave the cashier the exact amount of what the food cost. She proceeded to give me change back. I had to remind her that I had given her the exact change. It seemed to be hectic that night. Even after I told her that I was not due any change back, she still gave me $5 back. I tried to get her attention, but she did not hear me. So, after I received my food order, I drove around to the front entrance, got out of the car and went inside and told her that she had given me change that was not due me. She thanked me.

On my way out of the restaurant, one of the members from the church had stopped in to get food after service. He had another one of the members with him, and when he saw me, he gave me $20 to pay for my food. I told him that I had already paid for my food and was returning some over paid change. He told me to keep the $20 just because. Bishop Martin teaches on having integrity. My integrity was on the line.

Because I gave the $5 back that was **not mine**, God blessed me up and above the $5 through another individual, and I was able to buy my lunch the next day and have money left over. It pays to give your tithes and offerings. I even noticed that when I give offerings in addition to the tithes, I always have money in my purse. Bishop always teaches that when you give your tithes, you are only giving back to God what is rightfully His and only opening the windows of heaven. When you give your offerings, you cause blessings to flow through those windows.

Since our minister of music has been out on sick leave, I decided to take on the task of keeping the choir going. I am part of the music ministry, and when this ministry fails or flakes out, it's a reflection not only on the music department but also on our shepherds and our church. I don't believe God would be pleased with that.

Since I have taken on this task, God has truly been blessing me spiritually, physically and financially. Sometimes when the service is over on Sunday mornings, I am so elated and filled with God's spirit that I can hardly contain myself. I bask in the afterglow all week long and anxiously wait for the next Sunday to see what God is going to do through the music ministry. I am not a musician, nor do I know the musical notes or what keys the songs are sang in, but I use what God has given me to the best of my ability to try to make sure the music ministry is at least half decent. Praise be to God!

I encourage and exhort each and everyone to give your tithes and your offerings. It may seem like you cannot afford to give, but you also cannot afford **not** to give. God cannot lie—if He said to give and it shall be given back to you, good measure, pressed down and shaken over, men will give into your bosom, and however you give it out, it will be given back to you, He means just that! I am a witness that this particular verse is true. I trust God because he is my source and my provider—He is everything to me.

****

The abundance of joy experienced as a result of the manifestation of God's blessing can be felt when you read Sis. Jolly's testimony. This joy is available to all believers as God is no respecter of persons (Romans 2:11). He will do for one just as He will for another.

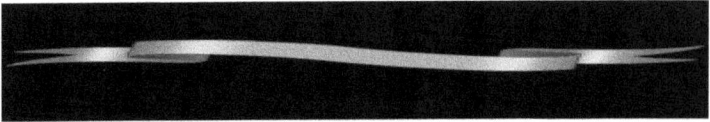

"Saintly Love"

"Am I my brother's keeper?"
Genesis 4:9

Two unconnected and unrelated men at a church desired to purchase clothing to wear to church, but both felt incapable of shopping on their own. Mr. Felderson, being the sharp dressed and kind-hearted man that he is, was approached by both men on separate occasions with a request to assist them in making their purchases. Mr. Felderson has a heart for men and was pleased to receive each request and just as happy to consent.

Upon receiving the invitations, Mr. Felderson scheduled an appointment to accompany each man to get his desired clothing. The happiness and warmth that was felt by the giver and the receiver was awesome. On each excursion, the men felt overjoyed as one was receiving the help he needed while the other was giving the needed help. When the two men arrived at church with their new clothing, the smiles that appeared on their faces told every spectator the men felt like brand new men of God.

Mr. Felderson stepped outside of himself and heard the cries of his brothers-in-Christ. His brothers had a need, and he was able to fulfill it. He did not look for anything in return, but he did receive the joy of the Lord, which is his strength. God has many blessings in store for this man of God because he has the heart of a servant and he gives freely.

****

Mr. Felderson is a wonderful example of Hebrews 6:10, *"For God is not unrighteous to forget your work and labour of love, which ye have shewed toward his name, in that ye have ministered to the saints, and do minister."* Although Mr. Felderson did not assist the two men to obtain favor from the Lord, he will. God rewards those who voluntarily and cheerfully see to the need of others.

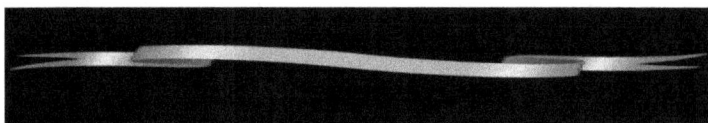

"Walking in Obedience"

Behold, to obey is better than sacrifice, and to hearken than the fat of rams."
I Samuel 15:22b

Approximately three years ago during the Easter season, Pastor Carlinda Lowery was directed by the Holy Spirit to give a resurrection offering. She had never planted a 'resurrection' offering before, but in obedience to the Lord, she did as she was told. She planted an offering of $400. Nearly one year later, in February, her eldest grandson, who was in his mid-twenties, was sitting in a parked car when the car door was suddenly opened. He was shot five times at close range.

When the police arrived to the scene, they discovered

he had been shot with a 9mm gun. However, when the doctors removed the bullets from various parts of his body, they noticed a different caliber bullet in his jaw. This confirmed he was shot with two different guns, most likely from two different shooters.

However, even with the bullets that penetrated his body (shattering one hand and one elbow) and those that grazed by his stomach and head, God spared his life and kept him fully conscious throughout the entire ordeal and the surgery that followed. When Pastor Lowery heard of her grandson's tragedy, she immediately thought back to her resurrection offering and had a full understanding of why the Lord placed it in her spirit to give. Because of her obedience, her grandson's life was spared.

****

Many times the Lord will impress upon us to perform a specific action or utter specific words, and we are left wondering why. Isaiah 55:8 says, "*For my thoughts are not your thoughts, neither are your ways my ways, saith the LORD.*" However, when we have a close walk with the Lord, as Pastor Lowery does, our spirits will be at ease when we are presented with such times. As a result, we too are able to walk in obedience with greater ease, as the peace of the Lord surrounds us.

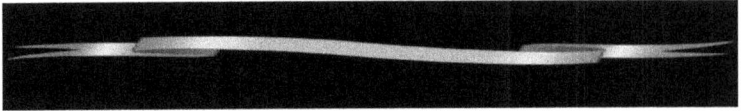

"A Godly Example"

"Ye are our epistle written in our hearts, known and read of all men."
II Corinthians 3:2

Evangelist Dorthea Johnson has been walking steadily with the Lord for the past ten years. During this time, the Lord has been cultivating her for various positions in ministry. Currently, she serves as armor bearer to the pastor's wife, vice president of the Special Events Committee, and president of the Book and Tape Department. In addition to holding these positions, she also assists others in their endeavors when requested. In particular, she has been very instrumental in International Women's Commission.

During her time of walking with the Lord and serving

in ministry, she has been growing and developing. Her family and friends have watched the light of the Lord grow brighter and brighter within her. Now, they desire to possess the same light, and they also want to be instrumental in the work of the Lord.

Evangelist Johnson gave her life and gives her service to the Lord. As a result, He gives her opportunities to be a witness, as a possessor of His light and a walking epistle being read of men.

****

There are many ways that we can be used of God. Once we avail ourselves unto Him, He will use us as He sees fit. Being used of God is an honor. We may not always agree with how we are used, but we must remember, it is all for the glory of the Lord.

"Making a Step Upward"

"My people are destroyed for lack of knowledge."
Hosea 4:6

While earning a master's degree, Cindy needed a baby-sitter for her two children, as all the graduate-level courses were only offered in the evenings when her children were not in school. Cindy could have taken only the early evening course and taken her children to the daycare on the college campus. However, this would have caused her to need twice as much time to complete her degree. The campus daycare was a godsend, but the hours did not extend to very late in the evening. She also could have taken the children to her mother's home or to her ex-husband's home, but neither of them lived close enough for travel time to and from school in the evening, plus Cindy did not want to ask for favors two to four times a week.

While attending classes, Cindy met Monica. Monica was gracious enough to offer to babysit the children while Cindy attended classes. What a blessing! What a load off Cindy's shoulders. What was even better was Monica lived only two blocks from the college campus. Cindy did not need to drive out of her way to drop the children off. Monica's house was on her route to school.

In return for Monica's generosity, Cindy helped Monica write her essays, as she was working toward a bachelor's degree and had difficulty understanding structure and analytical thinking. As time drew on, Cindy and Monica became very close friends and confidantes. Today, Cindy continues to assist others with their writing as well. This is her way of giving back.

Just recently, as Cindy reflected back on her time of study, she thought, "Where would I be today without my friend?"

****

So often, we overlook the kindness of others who go out of their way to assist us in our endeavors. We must always be cognizant of their kindness and say, "Thank you," because they have made a positive difference in our lives. We should stop and ask ourselves, "If it were not for the generosity in their hearts would the outcome of our lives be the same?"

"Compassionate Beautification"

"A generous man will himself be blessed."
Proverbs 22:9a (NIV)

Lamar Jones is a well-known stylist with extensive

clientele. All of his clients are well aware that they must make an appointment nearly a month in advance because his schedule has a tendency to fill very quickly. Mr. Jones, who is very charismatic and loves to joke, truly has a giving heart. When he has free time, and even when his time is not so free, he takes time to bless others. He blesses friends and loved ones in a variety of ways. Primarily though, he blesses others by using his gift as a stylist.

For example, one evening, after a full day of work, Stanley, a long-time friend of Mr. Jones, called and asked if Mr. Jones could come over to Stanley's home and style Stanley's daughter's hair. Even though Mr. Jones was exhausted from a full day of standing on his feet and creating beautiful hair designs for his clients, he consented to his friend's request. Not only did he leave the salon and drive to his friend's home, he also took all the necessary products and tools with which to style the little girl's hair. He did this free of charge from the compassion of his heart.

This kind act is only one of many. Mr. Jones often gives discounts to clients who have been with him for years and continue to get their hair styled on a consistent basis. Outside of the salon, he blesses family members and friends through monetary giving, and he even serves in his church, in the youth department when there are fashion shows or talent shows. All of his actions demonstrate that he is truly aware that it was the Lord who blessed him with his gifts and talents.

In return for his acts of kindness, Mr. Jones has been blessed to have his needs met on a consistent basis. He virtually wants for nothing. If ever there is a time of need, not much time elapses when God meets the need. And for this, Mr. Jones is truly grateful.

****

All of us have been blessed with talents. We must be mindful that the Lord requires faithfulness of His stewards (I Corinthians 4:2). Being faithful does not mean using our talents only when it suits or benefits us. It means using them when the need arises. Also, we must understand the talent truly belongs to the Lord; we are simply the vessel in which the talent is housed.

"Obedience is Better than Sacrifice"

"For I know the thoughts that I think toward you, saith the
LORD, thoughts of peace, and not of evil, to give you an expected
end."
Jeremiah 29:11

Every year, a popular California church hosts the Annual Living Word conference. In preparation for the conference, the choir takes on new growth, as church members temporarily become a part of the choir to enhance the impact of the conference. During one of the choir rehearsals that was held on a Tuesday night, the Holy Spirit spoke to one of the associate pastors and told him to buy a ticket for a person who was financially unable to attend the conference luncheon but who had a great desire to partake of the information that would be disseminated that day. In obedience to the Holy Spirit, the ticket was purchased and given to the person in need.

Approximately four months later, someone walked up to the associate pastor in church and gave him a Mercedes Benz at no cost to him. The only thought that resonated through the pastor's mind was, "You can't beat God giving no matter how you try!"

****

This testimony is not about the type of car that was given as a gift. Instead, it is about a need that was met through an obedient heart. The associate pastor did not have a car and secured rides from willing church members on a regular basis. With the car he was blessed with, the pastor can now hire a driver who can drive his car to take him where he needs to go. Philippians 4:19 says, *"But my God shall supply all your need according to his riches in glory by Christ Jesus."*

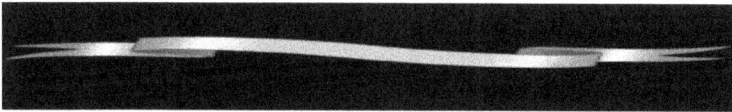

"Steadfast and Unmovable"

"Therefore, my beloved brethren, be ye stedfast, unmoveable, always abounding in the work of the Lord, forasmuch as ye know that your labour is not in vain in the Lord."
I Corinthians 15:58

A mighty evangelist suffered the misfortune of losing her husband in the prime of her life. His death caused a shift in the family. As a result, the evangelist had the complete responsibility of making sure the household needs were met. In an attempt to carry on, the evangelist found there was a shortage of finances to fulfill all the expenditures. As a mother of five young adult children, she was constantly helping them fulfill their obligations as well as paying the mortgage and the other household bills. Additionally at this time, the evangelist desired to place a new roof on the home.

One day as she walked outside to the mailbox, the Holy Spirit told her to turn around. As she turned, she was able to see the top of the family home through the trees. Then, Holy Spirit reminded her of His promise to her. He had told her that He would never leave her or forsake her. He also had told her that He would save her household.

As she looked back at her home, she reminisced about the words of the Lord. He had truly honored His word. Through all she had been through, He honored His word. When the house was in foreclosure, God had honored His Word. The evangelist did not lose her home. Her home continues to be a place of refuge for her children, grandchildren, and great grandchildren. She even received the new roof for the home.

God had done as He had promised. Every need had been met. Although the evangelist no longer had the company of her husband, she had the good fortune of knowing the Lord as her own personal Lord and Savior, and she had a relationship with Him.

****

The death of a spouse is unimaginable and disheartening, yet bearable. During this time, we may find ourselves in tough situations, but the grace and mercy of the Lord will continue to follow us all the days of our lives. We must allow God to order our steps and direct our paths. He knows which way is best for us to travel upon. Look to Him for guidance, for He will never leave us or forsake us (Hebrews 13:5).

"Singing Praises unto the Lord"

"Praise ye the LORD. Sing unto the LORD a new song, and his praise in the congregation of saints."
Psalm 149:1

Evangelist Carla Williams had a desire to praise the Lord in song, so she took part in a Christmas program at her church. When she opened her mouth to sing, the sounds that come forth were not what she had anticipated. She was not at all pleased with the outcome of her performance.

From that moment forward, she yet desired to praise the Lord in song, but she knew improvements had to be made.

A few years later, she had an opportunity to become a member of another church where she was able to have voice lessons. In addition, she learned how to hear tone and pitch. As a result of the lessons she was fortunate to have, her voice improved.

Another few years passed, and she returned to the church where the Christmas program had been held years before. She joined the choir and used her gift to praise the Lord. Not long afterwards, she was asked by the senior pastor to be the praise and worship leader. To honor the Lord and to fulfill the request of the pastor, she gladly took the position.

Now, Sunday after Sunday, she stands before the congregation and leads the praise and worship session ushering in the presence of the Lord.

Unfortunately, on one Sunday, Evangelist Carla took ill and was unable to go to church, much less lead praise and worship. Upon her return to church the next Sunday, several of the church members informed her that her presence and worship was truly missed. They told her how her ability to usher in the presence of the Holy Spirit allowed them to experience healing and deliverance. Oh, what a blessing!

In this instance, the cycle of giving came first from the Lord to Evangelist Williams. She was blessed with the gift of song. She, in return, gave her gift back to the Lord in service. As a result, the people, who, in addition to the Lord, are direct recipients of the gift, are blessed.

****

It has been said that the Lord works in mysterious ways. This particular blessing of song is one that continues to give every time the gift is rendered unto someone. The receiver is blessed and in return, the Lord is blessed.

"Godly Counsel"

"Only by pride cometh contention: but with the well advised is wisdom."
Proverbs 13:10

Evangelist Cathy Vines, an extremely anointed evangelist, who serves in a healing and deliverance ministry, was blessed with the friendship of two men of God who are both instrumental in their respective churches. One man serves as an elder, while the other serves as the minister of music.

What was ironic about the two new friendships that Evangelist Vines had developed was both men were encountering difficulties in their places of worship that caused them to question whether or not they would continue to serve in ministry in that particular church. Over two separate lunches, each man shared his experiences with the woman of God. As the spirit of the Lord allowed the men to pour out, Evang. Vines listened intently to the information that was being shared.

After hearing the details of the situations that each man was facing, with the leading of the Holy Spirit, Evangelist Vines began to minister life into the situation of each man of God. She spoke hope, faith, healing, and peace. Some time later, after having spoken into the men's life, the evangelist learned that each man remained faithful to his church. Even to this day, both are still serving faithfully in ministry.

As a result of Evang. Vines ministering and pouring into the lives of those she comes in contact with, God has continued to bless her ministry, allowing it to flourish and be a blessing to all those who are connected with it. The Lord has given the evangelist a place to hold services, so she can be a continued blessing to those that need to be delivered, healed, and set free from the holds that bind them.

****

These two situations could have gone awry. When the two men shared their accounts, the evangelist could have listened with her fleshly ears rather than her spiritual ears. Galatians 5:16 says, *"But I say, walk by the Spirit, and you will not gratify the desires of the flesh."* Because she listened with her spiritual ears, she was able to respond in the spirit and not in the flesh. Her offering of godly counsel saved the relationship each man had with his church. If the wrong counsel had been given, the men themselves could have been adversely affected by the outcome of their severance with the church.

Many people leave churches day after day. Some leaving is at the direction of the Holy Spirit while other leaving is not. Sometimes leaving causes a separation, not only from the church, but at times from God, due to the level of hurt a person may experience. We must be very careful when giving someone counsel regarding their church.

"The Power of Prayer"

"And he spake a parable unto them to this end, that men ought always to pray, and not to faint."
Luke 18:1

An elder of the church and his wife are members of an evangelical ministry that visits individuals on a monthly basis. One of the places that the couple frequents during their monthly visits is an assisted living home. They pray over all the residents who desire prayer. After months of visiting, the couple became relatively familiar with the owner of the home.

Recently, the owner, her husband, and her aunt were all in a car accident. While the husband was not badly hurt, his wife and her aunt required hospitalization. The wife, the owner of the assisted living home, suffered from a broken collar bone and a ruptured kidney and had difficulty walking. Her aunt suffered numerous injuries including head trauma; as a result, she fell into a coma. The doctors were hopeful about her condition, but they believed her recovery would be slow due to her being 80 years old and the amount of trauma her body sustained.

The accident occurred on a Sunday. On Tuesday morning, after undergoing numerous tests on Monday, when the wife was able to talk, she promptly called the elder and his wife to come to the hospital to pray for her and her aunt. Upon receiving the phone call and hearing the news, the couple immediately departed their home and headed for the hospital. After praying for the owner, the couple went upstairs to ICU to pray for her aunt.

After the couple made several visits to the hospital to pray, the owner was able to go home after being hospitalized for only one week. The aunt, who was in a coma, awoke sooner than the doctors expected but needed a tracheotomy. After the doctor inserted the trach, the aunt was moved from ICU.

After a few days of being in the regular patient room, the trach was removed. The elder and his wife showed up again for more prayer. They were told that the aunt would be unable to talk to them because she had just had the trach removed that very day. However, the aunt *did* speak, which was a surprise to the doctors. She told the elder's wife that she needed lip balm because her lips were dry. Soon afterward, the aunt was discharged early from the hospital. This too left the doctors in amazement. The doctors said all that occurred, after the couple prayed, were miracles.

****

Intercessory prayer warriors are people who intercede and pray on the behalf of others. They go before the presence of God without pride or other debilitating emotions and characteristics. They are clothed with humility, and they walk in the spirit of hope. They pull down strongholds and bind the hands of the enemy.

This is what the elder and his wife did on behalf of the car accident victims. God heard their cries and their prayers. Psalm 106 declares, *"Praise ye the LORD. O give thanks unto the LORD; for he is good: for his mercy endureth for ever."*

"Leaning on the Lord"

"God is our refuge and strength, a very present help in trouble."
Psalm 46:1

After a few years of being a member of a church, Clarita's friends, who were also members of the same church, decided to leave the church and place their membership elsewhere. Upon leaving, several of the friends invited Clarita to leave with them. Because the Lord had not instructed Clarita to leave the church, she did not.

A few months later, Clarita's mother passed away. This was a very rough time for Clarita, as it is for most people who lose a parent. As she was in her time of mourning, the Lord revealed to her how much she had grown from the time her friends left the church to the time of her mother's passing. By staying firmly planted at her church, the Lord was able to lay a solid foundation for her, where she could stand during times of trouble, such as dealing with her mother's death.

As a result of receiving God's blessing, Clarita continued to study her word, read her copy of *God's Promises*, and attend Sunday services and bible study. All of these activities allowed her to further her relationship with God. As a result, she began to pour out to others through prayer from what the Holy Spirit had poured into her. To date, she has helped people near and far, friend and stranger, through their times of trouble by praying for them. She has grown into a mighty intercessory prayer warrior for the Lord.

****

I Corinthians 15:58 says, *"Therefore, my beloved brethren, be ye stedfast, unmoveable, always abounding in the work of the Lord, forasmuch as ye know that your labour is not in vain in the Lord."* Many Christians can attest to being unmovable because they have been dedicated members of their church for years. However, can they say they have been always abounding in the work of the Lord?

Always abounding in the work of the Lord means you will not grow lazy in your service to the Lord, you will not let your feelings dictate when you will serve, nor will you let yourself falter in your commitment to reach the lost. How many can say this characteristic describes them?

The prayer warrior who shared her testimony can be found to be steadfast and unmovable in her commitment to the Lord. Also, she is always abounding in her attitude of prayer as she continues to pray for people everywhere she goes.

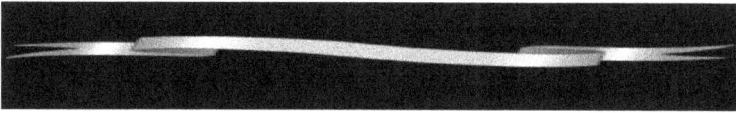

"The Art of Giving"
(The following testimony, shared by Rina Giron, is in her own words.)

God has blessed my life every day. At the right moment, He has provided me with many things that I needed. When we understand that the Lord is the possessor of all things and we are His stewards, responsible to Him for the way in which we manage what He entrusts to us, then we will understand the divide of the giving. What we have in our possession does not belong to us; everything belongs to the Lord. In exhorting us to give, He asserts in His words, *"Now He who supplies seed to the sower and bread for food will supply and multiply your seed for sowing and increase the harvest of your righteousness"* (2 Corinthians 9:10).

A good example of the giving in my life happened during the 2007 Easter season. I had been laid off of work since December 2006. I started looking for a job in January of the next year. I remembered that I had submitted a lot of applications, but no one called me for any interview.

As I cleaned the house, I found items we did not need that I could sell. Even after doing this, the money was still low. Slowly, I started to cook all the food in the house. One day, the only food left to cook were three bags of pasta. I decided to make spaghetti (without meatballs for I did not have meat for it) to feed the homeless. When I finished cooking, I went to feed them. They were so happy while eating.

When I went back home, I almost started crying because I found my kitchen without food. I remembered that I prayed and cried at the same time. One hour after that, somebody began to knock at the door. I went to open the door. A miracle was happening. A friend of mine, somebody that I never expected to do this, was opening his car's trunk and started to bring me lots of grocery bags. God had helped me again at the right time. He never left me alone; He never did.

****

When Rina found herself in a desperate situation, she did not turn away from God. Instead, she became like the widow who gave her all: her last two mites (Mark 12:42). Rina prepared the last food available in the house and fed it to those who were seemingly less fortunate. God, witnessing Rina's grace giving, immediately came to her rescue and replenished her cabinets and refrigerator. This is a demonstration of God's ability to do more than we ask or think (Ephesians 3:20).

"Giving and Receiving"

"But this I say, He which soweth sparingly shall reap also sparingly; and he which soweth bountifully shall reap also bountifully."
II Corinthians 9:6

(The following testimony, shared by Pat Calcagno, is in his own words.)

When I was asked to write a testimony describing how God has blessed me and how I have given back because of those blessings, I was at a loss. I can list all the blessings that God has given me, but I was ashamed that I couldn't just as easily list all the things that I have given back in return. Now don't get me wrong; I'm not saying that I haven't given back; I have. But, when you measure up all the gifts that I've been given and what I've given back, the scales seem woefully unbalanced. That was the dilemma I faced when I was asked to share my story, but once again God blessed me more than I deserved in the form of my college English professor, Dr. C. White-Elliott.

Dr. Elliott took the time to show me that I give more than I think I do. From the dollar I give the homeless man at the end of the off-ramp, to the time I spend with other students when I understand a concept and they don't, it's all giving. But I don't do it to get something in return; I do it because that's what God wants me to do.

I believe that God blesses me every day. He's blessed me with good health, financial stability and the opportunity to be back in school broadening my mind. Every day, He allows me to wake up, and He gives me the opportunity to try to be better than I was yesterday. I'm no saint, but I try to remember what Jesus said: *"Love each other as I have loved you"* (John 15:12), and every day I try to do something kind for someone.

Several years ago my mother was diagnosed with a serious lung disease. My parents were elderly, and my younger sister was living with them and taking care of them. The challenge of taking care of them was starting to take a toll on her, and she asked me to move back home to help out. I moved home, and my mother's health continued to deteriorate; at the same time, my father was diagnosed with early stage Alzheimer's disease. I was able to help take care of my mother until she passed away, and then I was there to help take care of my father until he passed away a few years later. I thank God that I was in a position to be able to help, and I truly believe that He blessed me with the gift of caring for my parents.

My giving has never been about money; it's about giving of myself. It's about doing something good for someone, especially someone I may not know. Jesus tells me that it's easy to love someone that loves me, so I try to keep my eyes open and look for that someone that I can affect, whether it's with some spare change or a couple of minutes of my time. I never thought it was much, but somebody showed me that in some cases it may be a life changing event for the other person.

****

Like Pat, we can all make a difference in someone's life. We should never discount a gift as being too small or meaningless. We never truly know the impact our giving has on someone's life, especially when that someone is a stranger and never has the opportunity to tell us. For all we know, we could have possibly fed someone who had not eaten in several days. We could have spoken words to someone giving him/her a ray of hope and stopped the act of suicide. What is important is our obedience to the prompting of the Holy Spirit. When He says move, we should move.

"Money has Nothing to Do with It"

"But seek ye first the kingdom of God, and his righteousness;
and all these things shall be added unto you."
Matthew 6:33

Andrea Johnson has always had a desire to teach, even when she was a young child. After earning her bachelor's degree, she elected to teach in Christian schools rather than in secular schools although the salary in secular schools is more favorable. In spite of the difference in pay, her heart was set on teaching in a Christian environment where she could teach the children everyday concepts along with the word of God.

As a Christian education teacher, Ms. Johnson was responsible for helping lay a godly foundation for her students, so she taught them how to pray and worship God. In exchange for giving the children what they needed to establish a healthy moral compass for everyday living, Andrea received the joy of seeing their growth and development.

As it relates to her income, God sustained Ms. Johnson in her finances. Although there may have been tough times throughout her life, God has seen her through each and every situation. She may have gone without some of her desires, but all of her needs and the needs of her children have always been met. For this, Ms. Johnson gives God all the praise, honor and glory that are due unto Him.

****

When God has a calling on our lives, it may not always fit into the financial scheme that we desire for ourselves. However, if we place the importance on fulfilling our innermost desire, which is our calling, rather than the financial compensation, God will make up the difference.

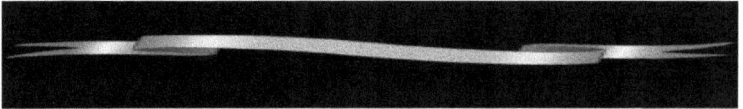

"A Servant's Heart"

"Therefore, my beloved brethren, be ye stedfast, unmoveable, always abounding in the work of the Lord, forasmuch as ye know that your labour is not in vain in the Lord."
I Corinthians 15:58

After knowing for some time that God had a calling on his life, four years ago James Johnson took a step to fulfilling his calling by beginning deacon training. After three years, James successfully completed the program and received his deacon's ordination. Now, as a faithful deacon of the church, Deacon Johnson is responsible for speaking into the lives of the children. He teaches both Wednesday night bible study and Sunday school for the youth. Deacon

Johnson is so dedicated to his calling and working with the youth that he also serves as a mentor for young men. Serving God through his deaconship, James is fulfilling his calling by speaking into the lives of the youth.

Each week, he is enthusiastic about the possibilities that lay ahead. He loves working with the children and serving the Lord. Knowing that he is now walking in his calling is a blessing in and of itself.

****

The bible says in Proverbs 22:6, *"Train up a child in the way he should go: and when he is old, he will not depart from it."* Deacon Johnson has the honor and the privilege of engaging with the youth and laying a solid foundation for them with the word of God. The angels in heaven are rejoicing as day by day the fruit of Deacon Johnson's labor reveals itself.

Each of us has the responsibility of touching lives wherever we go along life's journey. Being able to speak into the life of a child is a blessing, and we should be careful to cherish it by not abusing or neglecting the opportunity.

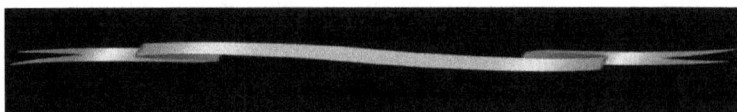

"All Needs Met"

"But my God shall supply all your need according to his riches in glory by Christ Jesus."
Philippians 4:19

Michael White placed his home furnishings into a storage unit when he moved out of his apartment until he located another suitable home for his family. During the time he was between apartments, his sister moved into her new apartment, but she was without a bedroom set. Michael graciously gave his bedroom set to his sister. A few months later, Michael located an apartment that suited his needs. Upon moving in, he was blessed with an apartment full of furniture (a living room set, a refrigerator, a dinette) and money to buy a new bedroom set.

****

Michael looked beyond his own need and met the needs of his sister. He trusted that God would supply his every need in due season. He was right!

"A Heart to Serve"

"For even the Son of man came not to be ministered unto, but to minister, and to give his life a ransom for many."
Mark 10:45

When Daron White was an eleventh grade varsity football player, he and his teammates wanted to do something to give back to the community. After discussing a few options, they decided to volunteer at the "Angel Food" food drive, every other Saturday, over the span of two football seasons. After having volunteered for the first four months, Daron was working diligently handing out food and a man, who had come to get food for his restaurant, walked over to Daron and handed him fifty dollars while saying, "I just wanted to give you this."

****

When we operate with a heart of compassion, God is pleased. He knows that we are not doing good deeds for what we may receive in return. Daron had no way of knowing he would be handed a blessing in the midst of giving back to his community. He was simply volunteering his time. But God saw the sincerity in his heart and allowed a blessing to come his way.

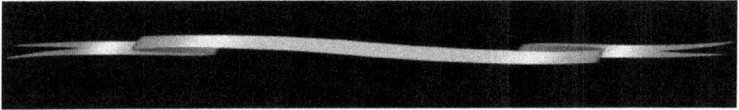

"Dedicated Service"

"Blessed is that servant, whom his lord when he cometh shall find so doing."
Matthew 24:46

Evangelist Flossie Carter is dedicated to the work of the Lord. Three to four days a week, she and a few other believers go outside the church and witness about the goodness of the Lord in an effort to win the lost to Christ.

Additionally, Evangelist Carter is a member of the church staff; she does various tasks around the church from cleaning, to preparing mailings, to decorating. She does it all unto the Lord and not for personal gain.

A few months ago, Evangelist Carter was without a car due to her car simply being run down. She was required to rent a car in order to have transportation. After renting cars for a few months, the Lord blessed her to be able to purchase another car. Having a vehicle of her own allows her to be more flexible with being able to serve the Lord in and out of the church building.

****

God does not forget our labor of love. He knows our needs. Philippians 4:19 says, *"But my God shall supply all your need according to his riches in glory by Christ Jesus."* Evangelist Carter's testimony is an example of the Lord's faithfulness.

Final Thoughts

After having read all the testimonies of God's goodness, it is my prayer that hearts and mindsets have been altered from being self-absorbed to being concerned with our fellow man. It is not only in the best interest of others, but it is in our best interest as well.

When we see to the needs of others, there are several benefits: we have less stress about our own situations because we are not consumed by them, we open our hearts to give love and to receive love, and we are encouraged because we know that we are walking in our purpose. Seeing to the needs of others is uplifting in so many ways because there are blessings received on both sides: the side of the giver and the side of the receiver.

This is God's plan for us. His word tells us in James 2:8 *"If ye fulfil the royal law according to the scripture, Thou shalt love thy neighbour as thyself, ye do well."* Our doing well is receiving God's blessing flow. Allow the blessing flow to flow into your life today and those of your loved ones by being a giver.

Gift of Salvation

for

Non-Believers

"For all have sinned, and come short of the glory of God."
Romans 3:23

This section was written especially for non-believers, those who have not accepted the gift of salvation. The gift of salvation saves souls from eternal damnation and is a free gift offered by God himself. John 3:16-18 says, *"For God so loved the world, that he gave his only begotten Son, that whosoever believeth in him should not perish, but have everlasting life. For God sent not his Son into the world to condemn the world; but that the world through him might be saved. He that believeth on him is not condemned: but he that believeth not is condemned already, because he hath not believed in the name of the only begotten Son of God.*" This section of scripture tells us God's purpose for giving His son Jesus to the world. The world was in a bad condition. The world was overwrought with sin; the people were living for fleshly desires rather than for God's desires.

As a result of the world's conditions, God decided that He would bring the perfect sacrifice that would save the world from being a place where people were lost and had no hope. He decided that His own son could stand in proxy for the sin-filled world, taking all sin upon Himself.

So Jesus came, born of a virgin, to save this dying world. He walked on this earth for 33 ½ years, doing the work of His Heavenly Father. At the appointed time, He died by way of crucifixion upon a cross at Calvary, on Golgatha's hill. He shed his blood and died for you and for me. Because His blood was pure, it cleansed the world of all unrighteousness and gave those who believe in Him direct access to His father's throne.

Scripture tells us in Matthew 27:51 that the veil of the temple was ripped in two from top to bottom, at the moment that Jesus' spirit left His body. As a result of the veil's removal, we are no longer required to have a high priest make intercession for us. We, as the children of the

Most High God, are able to approach God for ourselves, and Jesus sits on the right hand of the Father making intercession for us.

But what is even more miraculous than God offering His own son as the perfect sacrifice was the fact that when Jesus was placed in grave clothes and placed in a tomb, He only remained there until the third day. God would not have it that His son would remain in the heart of the earth forever. In order for people to believe in the awesome power of God and His dear son Jesus, a miracle had to be performed. So, on the third day, after Jesus died on the cross, He was resurrected, demonstrating the omnipotence of God. This very act was the act that would cause people to believe in a god that reigns supreme and holds the power of the universe in His very hands, a god that could save them from themselves.

Today, if you are an unbeliever, you can change your destiny. You can change where you will spend your eternity. Our Heavenly Father gives us the freedom of choice about how we want to live our life here on earth and how we want to spend eternity. In Deuteronomy 30:19, God boldly declares, *"I call heaven and earth to record this day against you, that I have set before you life and death, blessing and cursing: therefore choose life, that both thou and thy seed may live."*

So, dear friend what choice will you make today? Will you spend your eternity with the Creator or will you suffer Hell's eternal flames? Again, the choice is yours. Just as the men aboard the ship who were with Jonah became believers, you too can make a choice to accept the only one and true living God as your god.

If after reading the above passages, you have decided that you want to spend your eternity in Heaven with God, the creator, and His son Jesus, and the Holy Spirit, read through what has affectionately come to be known as the Roman's Road. This is the road to salvation. As you read through the scriptures that comprise the Roman's Road, you will also read the explanation for each scripture so that you will have clarity about what you are reading and confessing.

The Roman's Road to Salvation

The road to salvation begins with Romans 3:23 which declares, *"For all have sinned, and come short of the glory of God."* This scripture explains that everyone has come short of God's glory and needs redemption. Then Romans 6:23a states, *"For the wages of sin is death."* Here we learn that the consequence of living a life of sin is death. Everyone will experience physical death as a result of the sin committed in the garden of Eden, but those who commit themselves to a life of sin will suffer eternal damnation in the lake of fire (Rev. 19).

Continue with the rest of verse 6:23 that says, *"but the gift of God is eternal life through Jesus Christ our Lord."* There is an alternative to suffering eternal damnation. We can accept the gift of salvation by accepting Jesus as our personal lord and savior. Then, Romans 5:8 says, *"But God commendeth his love toward us, in that, while we were yet sinners, Christ died for us."* We are able to receive the gift of salvation because Christ came to earth and shed His blood for us on the cross.

Continue to Romans 10: 9-10 which says, *"That if thou shalt confess with thy mouth the Lord Jesus, and shalt believe in thine heart that God hath raised him from the dead, thou shalt be saved. For with the heart man believeth unto righteousness; and with the mouth confession is made unto salvation."* If we confess with our mouths that Jesus is the son of God, that he came and died for our sins, and that God raised Him from the dead, we will receive salvation.

Finish with Romans 10:13, which states, *"For whosoever shall call upon the name of the Lord shall be saved."* Call upon the name of God by saying these words, **"Lord Jesus, come into my heart and save me Lord. I believe that you are the Son of God who came and died on the cross for my sins. I believe that you rose from the grave. I also believe that you now sit in heaven on the right side of the Father, making intersession for me. I accept you as my Lord and my Savior."**

Now that you have confessed with your mouth that Jesus is the son of God and that He died for our sins and rose from the grave, **YOU ARE NOW SAVED!!!!** You will spend your eternity in heaven.

The next step is very important- you must find a bible-based church that teaches the word of God and confesses the Lord Jesus Christ to be the son of God. Don't delay. Do this immediately. Do not leave yourself open to the enemy. Get connected with the saints of the Most High God and keep yourself covered with the unspotted blood of the lamb.

Here is my prayer for you.

Father God,

I thank you for the opportunity to minister your word to the unsaved, the unchurched, and the uncommitted. Father God, I pray now for the souls who have just received the gift of salvation. Lord Father, they have opened their hearts to you, and I know that you have received them into your kingdom and written their names in the Book of Life. Father God, I pray that you will touch their lives and show yourself mightily before them. Let their eyes be opened by the scales falling off, allowing them to see clearly.

Father God, I even pray for the backslider, those who have turned away from you after receiving the gift of salvation. You said in your word that you desire that none would perish. So Lord, I send your word to them right now praying that they would confess the iniquity in their heart, repent, and turn from their evil ways, so that they may receive a life of abundance. You said in your word in Matthew Chapter 14, that every knee shall bow before you and every tongue will confess that Jesus is Lord.

Father God, I pray now that we all come under subjection to your word and that we will humbly submit

our lives to you. I ask all these things in the name of my Lord and Savior Jesus Christ.

Amen, Amen, Amen!!!!

I will continue to pray for your success in your walk with God. Remember, this spiritual walk that you are about to embark on will not be an easy walk, but remember, the race is not given to the swift but to those who endure to the end.

Be blessed with heaven's best. I love you!

ABOUT THE AUTHOR

Dr. Cassundra White-Elliott resides in California with her family. As an English/Education professor, she teaches for various community colleges and universities.

When writing, she writes with the direction of the Holy Spirit, in an effort to share with God's people all that He has for them.

In addition to teaching and writing, Dr. White-Elliott also serves as an evangelistic teacher. She is also the founder of International Women's Commission, a ministry that serves the needs of the entire person, by attending to healing the mind, body, soul, and spirit.

Dr. White-Elliott holds a Ph.D. in Education, a Master's in English Composition, and a Bachelor's in Education. Both education and writing are her passions. In addition to sharing God's word, she is the founder and CEO of CLF Publishing, Inc.

For your publishing needs, go to www.clfpublishing.org.

OTHER BOOKS BY THE AUTHOR

From Despair, through Determination, to Victory!

A lot can happen during a span of 40 years. The life of Dr. Cassundra White-Elliott has been anything but uneventful. From a fun-loving childhood sprinkled with incidents of abuse to a tumultuous young adulthood to a stable, secure adult life, she has experienced a full life, with much more to come. Her story is inspiring and motivating.

If anyone lacks hope, reading Dr. White-Elliott's autobiography will propel him/her into an attitude of "Maybe I can." This attitude, if nurtured and developed, will grow into an attitude of "Yes, I can." Throughout her life, Cassundra has always held in her heart the belief that she could achieve anything that she had a made-up mind to embark upon. She was determined to achieve her heart's desires, doing what God has called her to do. She takes no credit for herself. All the glory goes to God, for He is her driving force. In Him, she lives, moves, and has her being.

Through the Storm

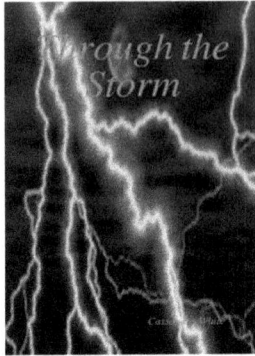

Preview

Through the Storm was duly inspired by the avaricious cloud of depression that decided to hover overhead of my daily existence in the latter part of 2007. Although I found it extremely difficult, I was once again compelled to not be defeated by just another snare that the enemy, the trickster, set for me. Once again, or more appropriately I should say *continuously*, he has exerted pernicious efforts to snatch the very life out of me by causing me to wallow in despair and to believe that I had been overcome by failure when in actuality and all reality, I was just experiencing a temporary set back. During those cloudy days, I had to remind myself daily that even though I was a target of the enemy, I am and will always be a child of the Most High god, Jehovah, who is my rock, my stability.

In my last book ***Dare to Succeed by Breaking through Barriers***, I discuss many barriers people find themselves faced with and the keys to successfully breaking through and overcoming those barriers. However, upon the release of the book, I too found myself faced with barriers, barriers in their multiplicitous form. Just as I reminded my readers, I had to continuously remind myself that one of the benefits of being God's child is the ability to be victorious in all battles, which comes from standing firm and continuing to fight the good fight of faith believing that I am an over comer and a conqueror as told to me in Romans 8:37.

During the midst of these seemingly perilous times, a dear friend gave me a cd by the Williams Brothers. While driving and listening, tears streamed from my eyes as I listened to the words of one particular song, "Still Here." The song says,

Heartaches, I've had my shares of heartaches, but I'm still here
Trouble, I've seen my share of troubles, but I'm still here
Bruises, I've taken my lumps & bruises, I but I'm still here
Loneliness, I've had my share of loneliness, but I'm still here

Through it all I've made it through another day's journey, God kept me here
I've made it through another days journey, God kept me here
Lied on, many times I've been lied on, but I'm still here
Burdens, I had to bare so many burdens, but I'm still here
Dark days, I've had my share of dark days, but I'm still here
Disappointments, I've had so many disappointments, but I'm still here

Chorus
It's by the grace of God, that I'm still here today

He was always there, no matter what came my way
I felt the presence of him, in my time of need
Standing right there, just to seal my faith

Chorus
I made it (I made it)
I made it (yes, I made it)
I'm still here (I'm still here)
A lot of folks say that I wouldn't be here tonight, but I made
it (I made it)
By the grace of God , yall (yes, I made it)
I'm still here (I'm still here)

I have to lay awake in the midnight hour sometimes, tossing
& turning (I made it)
All night long (yes, I made)
Have anyone had to lay awake all night long sometime (I'm
still here)
Tears in your eyes wandering what the next day was gonna
bring (I made it)
God kept has arms around you, yes he did (yes, I made it)
You made through the trails (I'm still here)

Come on let me see those hands in the air
I made it, I made it (I made it)
I made it, I made it (yes, I made it)
I made it, I made it (I'm still here)
Through it all (through it all I'm still hereeee)

To me, every word uttered in this song exemplified both
my past and present experiences. But the triumph in it all

was the victory that was in my grasp. I knew that I had to praise my way through to a new season.

But before victory was attained, with all the burdens that weighed heavily upon me, day after day I seemed to sink further and further, deeper and deeper into an abyss of depression. I fervently tried to shake it. But to avoid the daily pressures, that my life was consumed with, I would sleep later and later each day, in an attempt to avoid the world at large, which seemed to want to swallow me whole. This continued to the point where I would even turn the phone off to avoid not only the insolent bill collectors but also loved ones. I didn't avoid loved ones because I didn't love them any longer. No, I avoided them because I did not want them to hear in my voice the anguish I was enduring.

The irony of it all, though, was that I believed the word of God, and I knew unequivocally that He had not forgotten me and that he would not forsake me, for He had given me a life of blessings and he had already shown me glimpses of a very bright and promising future.

Unleashed Anger, Anger Unleashed

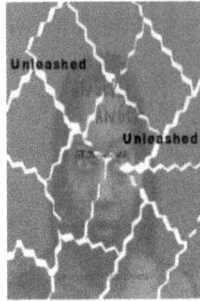

Preview

Introduction

What Is This Book All About?

As I prepared to embark upon the adventure of writing this book, I had to prepare myself to also be transparent. I have found that being transparent is required in order for healing to transpire, healing for all those that peruse the pages of this book and myself. And I may as well tell you that today, at the onset of this project, I have not been totally delivered from my condition of being an anger-filled person. However, I am definitely a work in progress. I have made strides with the assistance of my Lord and Savior, Jesus Christ, who is the head of my life. Without his love, guidance, and teachings, I would not be the woman of God I am today. I shudder to think where I could be instead and will therefore not entertain the thought.

Rather, I will confess that it is my desire that a transformation will result as I do an in-depth exploration of who I started out as when I was a little girl, the woman I became, and the woman that I am striving to be. It is my endeavor to see God tear down walls that encapsulate both my mind and soul and free me from the bondages of anger. It is my prayer that total deliverance will come between the writing of this sentence and the very last one of the book.

So, it is at this point that I must stop and utter a word of prayer.

Oh Heavenly Father,

I just want to stop and take another moment to give you praise, honor, and glory for being just who you are. You are the Alpha and the Omega. You are the finisher of my faith, for you knew my beginning before I departed from my mother's womb and you know my ending as well. Father God, I just want to thank you for your grace, the grace that you have afforded me, oh Lord, to still be here and to be able to tell my story. A story that will set captives free, present company included. Father God, I just want to tell you that I love you because you love me in spite of me. You love me with all my imperfections. You love me because as it says in your word that I am a royal priesthood. I am the daughter of the Most High God; I am the daughter of the King of Kings. Father God, I thank you for your love and the strength to be able to cause this work to come to manifestation. Oh Lord Father, I humble in your sight. I place my face to the ground and cry out your name. I cry out for healing in the name of my Lord and Savior, Jesus Christ. I believe that you will give me favor and grace to heal and to let your glory reign mightily in my life. So, therefore I place my life back into your hands, so that you can do a mighty work. I enter this prayer in the name of your son, Jesus Christ.
Amen.

Readers, as the writing of this book takes me through my transformation, I pray that the reading and re-reading of it will take you through yours. If you desire to be free, as I do, remember freedom can be yours. It is a gift for believers of the Almighty God. We just need to first believe that we can be free, pray for freedom, receive our freedom (by the necessary path as revealed to us by the Holy Spirit), and then confess with our mouths that we are free and are no longer bound.

Dare to Succeed by Breaking through Barriers

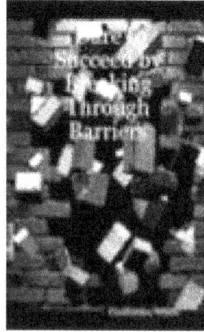

Preview

Introduction

Over the past few years, while conversing with family, friends, associates, strangers and even my students, I have noticed a common pattern amongst believers and non-believers alike. In both groups, there are those who make things happen because of the belief system they live by, and there are others who tend to demonstrate debilitating thoughts about the very course of their lives. Those who demonstrate debilitating thoughts do not seem to believe that their destiny is controllable. They tend to believe that whatever is supposed to happen will happen- on its own. As a result of this type of thinking, they don't put much effort into the outcome of their future, or should I say not as much effort as they could. For non-believers, this attitude and behavior is understandable because some non-believers are driven by their own self will while others have a lack of self will and are, therefore, not driven at all. But for believers who have the word of God, as a guide for their lives, I call this attitude living a substandard life compared to the one that God planned for His children. This is a result of failing to tap into the inheritance that God himself promised believers in His holy word.

Living a substandard life simply means living below one's capabilities. Many people believe that it is the set of talents each of us has been gifted with that enables us to be productive and live a prosperous life. Although our talents and how we use them have much to do with our earthly success and will lend to our prosperity, for believers our talents are not our only resources. God is our source for prosperity and He dispenses it to us. That is not to say that there are not varying levels of prosperity because there are and just like grace it is not dispensed by God evenly amongst men.

However, there are many believers who have failed to tap into the very essence of their beings. They are not tapping into their God-given talents nor are they using the power of prayer to tap into the prosperity that God desires for His children. The bible tells us that, *"the effectual fervent prayer of a righteous man availeth much"* (James 5:16b). When people live below their capabilities, they are not doing everything within their power to live a prosperous and fulfilled life. In many cases, there is one explanation for why we live below our means. Outside of the reasons of just not caring or being unaware of the word of God, in many cases there are barriers that stem from the past that block prosperity and prevent us from moving ahead into the future that God has designed for us.

For non-believers, whatever is in their physical, mental, financial, and educational power is what patterns their lives. Believers, on the other hand, have all these resources available to them with one added bonus. They have the power of the Holy Spirit available to them.

Public Speaking in the Spiritual Arena

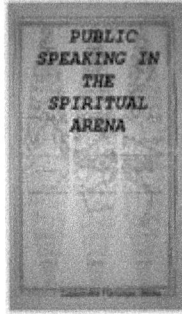

Preview

Chapter Two
How Communication Works

Purpose: This chapter will explain the six primary components of communication, identifying their purpose and how they work together.

The Source

In oral communication, the source of information is the speaker. In a church setting, the foundation of the message is God's word, but it is a speaker's interpretation of God's word that is delivered to the audience. As speakers vary, the information may vary but should have a similar essence because the foundational text is the same.

The Message

The message is the collective set of ideas that the speaker (the source) wants to deliver and/or illustrate to the audience. The message can be informative where the speaker informs the audience about a specific set of information. Or, the message may be persuasive in nature if the speaker wants to persuade the audience about conducting themselves in a specific manner, accepting God's commandments, or any number of things.

The Audience

The audience is the person or persons who are to receive the message. In the spiritual arena, there are many instances where an audience is present. It may be a traditional worship service, bible study, a conference, or a meeting. In any case, those who are there to receive the message from the audience, regardless of the number of individuals.

Where is Your Joppa?

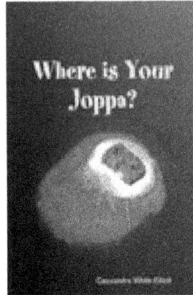

Introduction

Where is Your Joppa? was written for the express purpose of illustrating God's call for obedience in the lives of believers with respect to the individual call that He has on each of our lives. As you read throughout the various chapters, notice that the emphasis is placed on our persistent disobedience in answering God's call in a specific area of our lives. We have become a people who are similar to the Israelites when they found themselves in the middle of the wilderness, following their exodus from Egypt. Before God, they murmured and complained about their current life conditions and failed to be obedient to God's statutes delivered through His servant Moses. Their persistent disobedience caused them to lose the opportunity to see and enter the Promised Land. I ask you, "What has your disobedience cost you?" "Was your disobedience worth what it cost you?" "Do you think about the souls you could have ushered into the kingdom of God?" These are some of the questions that I pray will be answered through your reading of the book.

128

The first chapter following this introduction provides a detailed interpretation and analysis of the Book of Jonah, which serves as the foundational text for this book. Jonah, a prophet of God, commits an act of disobedience out of a spirit of pride and superiority. We, like Jonah, may also be afflicted with a spirit that prevents us from being obedient to God's call. Some of us are afflicted with pride, bitterness, unforgiveness, and rebellion, to name a few. These spirits are direct impediments to our obedience. However, others may not be afflicted with a spirit at all. We may be operating out of ignorance, not knowing that what we *are* doing is preventing us from what we *should* be doing.

Following the exegesis, the next three chapters (2-4) will provide examples of people today who walk in a spirit of disobedience. Using the theme "Joppa," I will pinpoint various situations that have occurred in the lives of several individuals that served as impediments to answering God-given mandates. What you may find surprising is that particular situations, relationships, or tasks that we may deem as honorable may indeed be impediments *if* we have allowed them to become a means of escape from what God has called us to do. So the situations themselves are not negative, but when we allow them to supersede God's call, our actions become negative. Reading these scenarios will prepare you for chapter five.

Chapter 5 discusses the necessity to perform a self evaluation. In order to see whether or not our lives indeed need to be turned around, we must be honest with ourselves about whether or not we have run from the call of God and situated ourselves in a safe haven, our very own "Joppa." When we honestly examine ourselves and allow the Holy Spirit to show us what lies deep within the recesses of our hearts, we provide ourselves with an opportunity to get our lives in order. Whether or not we actually make a change is something all together different.

After doing an honest assessment of our spiritual walk with God and unveiling any hidden "Joppas," we have to determine the right time to walk in obedience. Everyone has his/her own season for doing what God has mandated. Some of our seasons are right now, and some of our seasons are in a time to come. Knowing the right time to move is just as important as answering God's call. Therefore, Chapter 6 will discuss God's timing for us to move and for us to be still.

Finally, during the writing of this book, the Holy Spirit led me to appeal to the unbeliever. Chapter 7 is directed to the unbeliever, providing an opportunity for salvation.

As you read through the various chapters of the book, I pray that you will be receptive to the written words on the pages that were written under the direction of the Holy Spirit, as well as the words the Holy Spirit will undoubtedly speak directly to you about your own situation. Finally, do not hesitate to share this book with those whom the Holy Spirit leads you to.

I pray that the spirit of fear will not entrap you.

I pray that you will yield yourself as a willing vessel to our Heavenly Father.

I pray that you will answer the call that God has on your life.

Remember, I Samuel 15:22b states, "To obey is better than sacrifice."

www.ingramcontent.com/pod-product-compliance
Lightning Source LLC
Chambersburg PA
CBHW072026040426
42447CB00009B/1758